PALM CROWS

Camino del Sol

A Latina and Latino Literary Series

PALM CROWS

Virgil Suárez

The University of Arizona Press

Tucson

The University of Arizona Press
© 2001 Virgil Suárez

♾ This book is printed on acid-free, archival-quality paper.
Manufactured in the United States of America
First Printing

06   05   04   03   02   01   6   5   4   3   2   1

Library of Congress Cataloging-in-Publication Data
Suárez, Virgil, 1962–
Palm crows / Virgil Suárez.
p. cm. — (Camino del sol)
ISBN 0-8165-2099-2
1. Cuban Americans—Poetry.   2. Cuba—Poetry.
I. Title.   II. Series.
PS3569.U18 P35 2001
811′.54—dc21   00-012204

British Library Cataloguing-in-Publication Data
A catalogue record for this book is available from the British Library.

Publication of this book is made possible in part by the proceeds of a permanent endowment
created with the assistance of a Challenge Grant from the National Endowment for the Humanities,
a federal agency.

For Gabriela,
Wild Child of Beautiful Spirit

Contents

III *Duende*

Acknowledgments

I would like to thank Ryan G. Van Cleave for his dedication, editorial expertise, and friendship. Also, for the inspiration and words of encouragement: Bruce Weigl, Jim Daniels, Allison Joseph, Denise Duhamel, Angela Ball, Bryce Milligan, David Baker, Margot Schilpp, Kathleene West, Ray Gonzalez, Leroy V. Quintana, Yusef Komunyakaa, C. Dale Young, Timothy Liu, Christopher Davis, Victor Hernández Cruz, Alberto Ríos, Orlando Ricardo Menes, Ricardo Pau-Llosa, Gustavo Pérez Firmat, Jeff Knorr, Wasabi Kanastoga, Andrei Codrescu, and Rodger Kamenetz.

An individual artist grant from the Florida State Arts Council helped tremendously in the completion of this book. I would also like to take this opportunity to thank Patti Hartmann at the University of Arizona Press for her generosity of spirit with this book, and the wonderful staff at the press for their hospitality and support.

Finally, a special thanks to my wife and daughters (the loves of my life) and family who provided the understanding and time to allow me to write in peace.

PALM CROWS

Palm Crows

in Hialeah where my mother lives her life
as a widow, each year the crows flock

and gather everywhere—the branches of trees
sag heavy under their communal weight

as they burst heavenward at the slightest
provocation from noise in parking lots,

or banks of canals—everyone hates
them, especially old Cuban men,

those birds of black luck, aerial doom—
nuisances all as they splatter cars with crap,

the males do this gawkish dance circling
the duller females, wings stretched as in mock

longing, an empty embrace—their screech
fills Hialeah afternoons with the despair

of exile, of absence, memories of days past,
captured cities, lost love, claimed lives.

Outside La Carreta Restaurant, the strongest
males perch on the fronds of Royal Palms,

black monks, resilient, darkened with penance
as they wait for crumbs, for a chance to eat.

Here they gather and roost long into the night,
and during the middle of these humid hours,

the Cuban children dream of plucking crows,
like fruit, at first ripe and sweet, then rotted,

poisoned with the bitter aftertaste of exile,
these worms that burrow into their lives

and which they will come to know well
in this new home where palm crows rise again.

I

Animalia

Carp

This time last year, late October,
my father (still living) came to Tallahassee,
and we went fishing at the small lake
near the house. We sat in the crisp
day by a solitary pine's quiet stillness:
witnessed turtles kick up mud in underwater
clouds, tug our wormed hooks, and I realized
then how frail and thin my father had become.
A twig, a feeble branch any wind could
snap. Then his cork dipped quick under,
and he pulled and stood to hold the pole
steady, a smile on his face. He reeled fast,
and the fish—a ghostly luminescent carp—
broke the surface and swam ashore,
already having given up. My father held the fish
by its gills and asked how good it would taste.
No, I told him, nobody ate what
they fished out of this stagnant lake black.
Nobody. Well, he intended to take this baby
home and have my mother fry it up;
then the fish twisted out of his hand,
suddenly a splash, a flicker of shadow vanishing
in the murky depths, and my father grinned
because he knew we had shared a moment,
unlike so many others in our lives. This one,
like the vulnerability of the carp, hooked
in his memory, in mine, like some gold coin
catching a flash of light in the cool bottom.

Tiñosa

blackbirds, scavengers, they existed in Cuba
where people feared them, not only for their

love of carrion and carnage, but because they stood
for bad omens, many times I heard my father

call other people—bearers of bad news—*tiñosas,*
aves rapiñas. I only think of these birds when I'm driving

and I mistake ravens and crows pecking at roadkill,
for them. And when I think of these *tiñosas,*

I think of my father dying of a massive coronary
and of the great distance between Tallahassee

and Havana, Cuba, and I find myself gripping
the steering wheel, hands sweaty,

as if I'm holding on for dear life.

Animalia

As a child, the games to break boredom included a certain cruelty
   of which only children are capable. Plucked wings from flies,
      caught lizards & geckos, trapped fireflies in jars. I kept my distance
   from the frogs, which the other kids in the neighborhood, aware of my terror,
insisted on putting down the back of my shirt or pants. We caught

lagartijas with long grass stems & noosed them around their necks, then lowered
   the lizards into the black recess of a spider's hole—like fishing, the spider
      bit the lizards & dragged them down. The trick was to pull the spider out
   of its hole; then one of us would smash it with a rock. We hated
everything that crawled on so many hairy legs. Ants we fried using

a magnifying glass & the power of the sun. We encircled scorpions
   in a ring of kerosene & set fire to the ring to watch the insect sting
      itself in an act of suicide. Once, I slashed the tires of my brand new bike
   (a bicycle my father had stood in long lines to buy) & made a double-banded
slingshot, the best the kids in the neighborhood had ever seen or held.

They envied, all right. A group of us went out into the backyard to shoot
   sparrows. I killed my first as it perched on the clothesline, preening
      its feathers. The pebble from my slingshot broke its breast-
   bone, & it plummeted to the ground. Fueled
by the violence of those days, I became an expert at killing—I learned

from watching my father & uncles slaughter so many animals in our backyard.
   Pigs, chickens, goats, rabbits, turtles. The pigs my father knifed in the heart
      while they ran. "It's the only good way," my father would say,
   "so they don't squeal." The goats bleated & kicked as they hung by ropes
from a roof beam, necks about to be slashed in one swift motion,

their throats opened & so much blood flowing. Then the countless chickens
   & ducks & guinea fowl whose necks my mother wrung, lending meaning
      to "running around like a chicken with its head cut off." Rabbits, turtles,
   pigeons, turkeys, fish, from both the rivers & the ocean—all killed & gutted
in the eyes of so many children. Stray dogs followed me home from school, mangy,

filthy & hungry, but my mother wouldn't let me keep any as a pet. In those days,
as now, people would kill & eat anything in Havana, Cuba, & I think she feared
the temptation. We raised & kept animals in our yards. So did everyone else
in the barrio. Even after severe sanitation laws and fines, people took chances
& hid animals in their bathrooms, bedrooms,

closets. One time the military came to our neighborhood & confiscated
all the animals, rounded them up & led them to a huge pit dug by a bulldozer.
All the animals were herded into this pit & set on fire.
Ah, the carnage & the wail of so many burning animals. On school field trips
they took us to the chicken hatcheries & showed us how male baby chicks

were ground up to make feed for the zoo animals. My father was a *gusano*
then & made to work against his will as a killer of horses to feed the lions
& tigers at the zoo. He never confirmed the story about the baby-chicks-
ground-up-as-feed. He did tell us about the monkey that played & teased
a cage full of tigers until one day it slipped & fell, & the tigers quartered

it immediately. My father smuggled home some meat from the horses
he killed. There also were sexual-perversion stories told
by neighborhood punks—with goats, pigs, dogs, even chickens.
My father told me that when he was a kid & his uncle wanted to get him out of a
conversation, he'd send my father to *tentar las gallinas,* which meant that my father

went into the chicken coop & stuck his pinkie into the chicken's cloaca to feel
for the next-morning's egg. I had a bunny which a couple of fierce
neighborhood dogs caught & mauled. Cats, too, suffered
in our neighborhood. They died regularly in jute sacks hung from trees
& beaten like piñatas or left in bags on the railroad tracks.

Such cruelty makes the mind's-eye burn, the heart flutter . . . We fished
the rivers, roamed the woods for everything & anything
edible—doves, quail, even rats. When my parents sent me off
for the summer to San Pablo in the province of Las Villas, to my maternal
grandparents, it was no better, no escape from people & their slaughter

of animals. Within the context of a farm, the killing made sense,
        became less disturbing. I witnessed the castration (in cold blood) of pigs
                & bulls. My grandmother chopped the heads off guinea fowl.
        She set me the task of plucking the feathers & cleaning each bird. In 1970,
the madness stopped when we left for Spain, where the only animals were those

that people kept as pets. Of course there were the carcasses at the markets,
        but humans no longer killed & ate their pets—they didn't have to. I too kept
                my first animals as pets: goldfinches, goldfish, hamsters, a turtle.
        I kept them throughout my youth in Madrid & later when we moved
to Los Angeles, California. After so many years I came to appreciate creatures

well-kept & alive. These days I have a dog (more on him later) & a garageful
        of canaries. I've become quite a canary culturist. During the breeding season
                it sometimes becomes necessary, because of genetic disasters,
        to dispose of a canary chick. Often, if things go wrong, a chick might be born
without a limb, or, as was the case recently, without eyes. To have to cull

is to return to the violence I experienced in my youth, but to leave
        such a creature in pain is unpardonable, so I cull, which means I push
                the chick into a glass of water. Recently, at a bird show I asked several
        bird keepers what humane methods they employ. The discussion turned
into a heated argument about the best way being no good at all, but the majority

of us agreed that to kill a bird quickly is to, like a chicken, snap its neck.
        The process by which this is done varies from the cruel & macabre
                to the quick & painless. Now about the dog, our basset hound, Sir Mongo
        of Tallahassee, who, though AKC registered, is far from being a
champion. Our dog. Our dog which has been howling & crying at night since

we brought him home as a puppy. His nocturnal whimpering & wheezing
        are enough to test anyone's patience, & I won't mention his lack
                of intelligence. Sometimes when he can't stop crying, I get out of bed,
        naked or clothed, & I walk to the kitchen to plead with the dog for a little
silence, a little rest. But it is no use. He whimpers & cries more. We keep him

behind a gate in the kitchen, & when he isn't making noise, he is busy making
     mischief. He will search & destroy almost anything he can reach, from cereal
          to fruit, from thawing meat to coffee. It's worse when we have visitors. He
     once stole David Kirby's glasses & chewed, possibly ate, glass & plastic—we
found only half of the frames. But the nighttime is the worst,

& so there's nothing to do but rage. Once I let myself hit Sir
     Mongo of Tallahassee with a rolled-up newspaper, & he stopped,
          but only briefly to catch his breath. It was during this moment that I
     glimpsed a reflection of my half-naked self in the window—a creature
nocturnal, like any, driven mad by lack of sleep. When I looked across the dark

expanse of yard, I saw a light in my neighbors' kitchen window.
     I imagined a person there, awake at the same hour, up for a glass
          of milk, & then, the same image I saw on my kitchen window, a big naked
     Cuban, rolled-up newspaper in hand, threatening to beat up his dog. No, not
easy to explain, the many years as witness & participant in the slaughter

& cruelty to animals. What would you think?

What Is the Poet Left?

For Richard Blanco and Pablo Medina

God? The river?

A bend in the river?

Exilios: or its stages for refugees?

A curtain billowing out the window?

An insect imprisoned in an empty glass?

The shimmer of the waves?

A blackbird on the horizon?

A watchfulness, felinelike

for what stands out in the distance?

White noise?

Grief & Melancholy?

Loss by association

in these bitter cold cities?

Absence & then rebirth?

A walk to bring out the memories

of another time, another place.

All that came before,

all that came after,

swallowed.

Chupacabras

When we moved to Tallahassee,
    my father always telephoned with a recap
of the morning news he read
    in *The Miami Herald* or listened
to on the radio; then he called in the late afternoon
    to chit-chat more, find out
if we needed anything. Sometimes I joked
    with him, sometimes my wife did.
One time he called at 3 A.M.
    to warn us about a strange creature,
half-goat, half-dog, hideously ugly
    with a forked tongue, red eyes,
covered with human hair, thirsty for blood,
    especially that of children
and small animals. We asked him
    what it was and he said:
Chupacabras, which literally means
    "goat sucker," and somehow he
made sense, and for a few days
    we don't let the girls play
in the yard or too far out of sight,
    and at night I stay awake, look
out windows at the expanse
    of darkened yard, out beyond
the pond where the frogs are calling,
    and the fog billows like a tent,
and shadows form and linger too long.
    Some people don't believe
in such creatures, but I'm standing
    here thinking about the possibilities
of such a beast existing when I completely
    forget about Mongo, our basset hound,
who looks, in the right conditions,
    like a half-pig, half-goat hybrid,

and he sneaks up on me and licks my toes,
    and then I feel the warm urine
against my leg—his, not mine. Still I think
    of all the curses, all the times in human
history when this has happened: a crazy
    idea allowed to blossom,
and quite suddenly I feel wide open,
    vulnerable, like any other nocturnal
beast, longing for survival,
    ready to believe in most things.

La noche

> *It is the light of houses in the distance*
> *punctuating the night.*
> —David Ignatow, "Night"

walking the dog in the dusk hours,
fireflies jump from the tall grass

as if to say hello, charm far-off mates
with their flash of longing, out again

on the path around the bend, past
the pond from where the frogs beckon ,

as though they await rain, and I think
of my father and how much he loved

the sound of frogs and rain falling
on the tin roof of our patio

in Havana when he would come home late
in the day, tired from killing horses

which he had fed to zoo lions; he would lay
on his jute-sack hammock that my mother

had sewed for him one birthday, and he would
fall soundly asleep, and I would sneak

up on him, because there were days
(and nights) when I would not see him,

and I would smell him, hear the rhythm
of his breathing and look down

his open mouth, a dark cavern in the fresh
night. And I thought one day my father

would swallow me, my aimless life,
and he does, tonight, he does, like a void,

like this walking into the evening
darkness when, as Hansel & Gretel,

I look upon the distant house lights
as those crumbs left behind, follow them

to find my way back to my own house.

Fake *Mariposa*

My mother arrived
in our new house,
where she walked
the distance
of the fenced yard,
and as she went
named every flower,
plant, tree, shrub . . .
as though they too
thrived in Cuba,
her homeland.
She named the plant
growing by the swing
and porch a *mariposa,*
Spanish for butterfly,
said it would flower white
in August. She left
and no flowers. Come
August, instead, green
artichoke-tipped
sprouts lanced tall
from the earth.
Still no flowers, neither
white nor yellow-gray
to attract hummingbirds
and bumblebees.
After the hurricane
season, the spearheads
turned red, ripe, fire
spears in the sunlight.
Mariposa or not,
this could be the plant
to bridge this life
with the secret soil
of the next.

Wind Rustles

the dead leaves
cross the lawn

tongue twisters
in Spanish & English

hojas muertas
it is spring

new leaves
poke through

on the dogwood
& maple

branches
birds perch

sing / *cantan*
love calls

mockingbirds
cardinals wrens robins

all asunder
here in Tallahassee

land of kudzu
Spanish moss pollen

casa / home
wind rustles

soft its blessing
the kiss of sky

sifts anew
everything

Poem for Jack Ridl

Toward the end of September,
duckweed blankets the pond's
surface, a verdant promise.

The turtles peek through for air,
dive under at the slightest provocation,
miniature Loch Ness Nellies.

Lizards scurry between the wisteria
bushes. There is room in this garden
for the violence of nature: a pair

of hawks, intent on rearing their
only chick, feed it a daily diet
of tree frogs and squirrels. Our dog

chases both up trees as if to save
their lives. The bullfrogs spawned
in the rainwater-filled wheelbarrow

by the garage; the tadpoles eat mosquito
larvae, then each other until only a few
remain, under the shade of the oak.

The clouds gather in the sky, hint
of the rain the new gardenia bushes
crave. I go daily to look out,

walk, get the mail, enamored
of everything that grows, crows,
the breeze's rapture caught among pines.

Coelacanth

prehistoric fish,
thought to be extinct,
blue-sheened,
long like barracuda,
the fish scholar
finds you thousands
of miles from where
you are supposed to be,
in a fish market,
sold by the pound;
there you
weighed in at 87 pounds,
green-eyed, dead
once more,
and the scientist
wants to send you
to his land, another
thousand miles
away, crated in ice,
your frozen body
on the slab, fingers
poking your once-supple
skin, a scale here,
an incision there.
Here you are simply
known as the "fish
that makes people
pass oil." There?
Well, there will be fame,
pictures, flashes of light
plenty to blind
the eyes for another
thousand years.

Grunion

One Saturday night the moon
    brought them to the shores
        of Seal Beach. I lay under a blanket

    with my date, naked except
    our underwear, her bra unhooked,
our lips sore from so much kissing,

our legs tangled in this frenzy of lovemaking,
    when out of the dark, flashlight
        beams dart the sand

    and we hear voices, the girl and I,
    her name not even a memory now,
and the voices, soft at first, are loud

in their approach, and we can't understand.
    I say Chinese, she says Russian,
        and we laugh because we don't

    know where we are, a little tipsy still
    from the dinner's wine, and the voices
now so close—Japanese men—and they are many,

silhouettes in the half-light, pants rolled up
    to their knees, and barefoot they kick
        at the wet sand all around us

    as they head out to where the tide
    ends, excited, they move about with buckets
into which they gather handfuls of grunion, slivers

of light reflecting off their scales, and the girl wants
    to go see so she puts on her clothes
        and walks over to join the men. I go

    in my boxer shorts behind her to the edge,
    where the water crashes over the sand,
and all around us fish braid in their spawning,

and we laugh and help gather the fish for these people
    we don't know, and all the time they are laughing
        with us, maybe at us, probably at my nakedness,

    and I kick up some water and splash them
    and they splash back, their buckets almost full
with these tube-thin fish, silver bars, currency

of this night, and as the fish fall into the buckets,
    they twist and flounder, and I can't help
        but want to free them so I run up

    to everyone with a bucket and turn the fish
    out, and they pull and call me crazy
in English, and it is that kind of night, filled with lunacy

and frolic for what secrets remain,
    so few, of nights like this one
        captured, released.

Pinkies

What they call baby mice or rats
    at the pet stores, these wriggle-
wiggle, peanut-shaped, furless
    creatures, alien (almost),
boa constrictors' and monitor
    lizards' food.
These places advertise "feeding times"
    on their shop windows,
and sure enough people gather
    to witness a clerk jiggle
a dead pinkie, tease the snakes
    to a first bite-grab-coil,
bite, grab, coil—the masses
    so easily entertained.
The moral of this poem,
    with a twist, is one day
a full-grown boa, sixty-five feet
    in length, nuzzles
through its wire mesh cage,
    grabs the leg of a juicy clerk,
balls him up in its coil of ever-
    tightening skin
& corkscrews out his
    breath, a gasp at a time.
The attendant's cry is inaudible
    over the crush of bones, &
people on the other side of the glass
    window are hypnotized, amazed
by the attendant-gone-limp.
    Stupefied, they can't decide:
911 or shout encore?

Cuys

A man from the Andes moved to a New York
    suburb and decided to raise guinea pigs,
built a *cuyero* house, similar to a thatched
    kitchen in a hut back home. His intention
was to have *cuy* meat available for special
    occasions, summer barbecues, also because
the animal's noises, purrs, and clicks, pleased
    him, helped him stave off homesickness.
On warm days, the man let the animals graze
    in the garden; one afternoon he forgot
to feed them, and the pigs wandered into the streets,
    unable then to find their way home,
and when the temperature dropped, they all died
    of hypothermia. The man, unable to contain
his sadness, drank himself silly, lost in his second-
    hand clothes. He moped about, aimless,
poor, his longing for home like the furry balls
    that wandered into Manhattan's flower district
where a woman carrying groceries saw one,
    a creature she swore looked like a giant rat.
She screamed and let go her groceries,
    a huge rat who stopped her to ask for directions.

Urchins

In the Havana of my childhood, when I was six,
    my father took me by bus to the beach.
My mother packed us a travel bag with our towels,

some sandwiches, crackers with homemade
    mango jam, a change of clothes. We rode
the loaded diesel bus—he holding onto my hand,

saying *lata de sardinas,* me pressed against the bodies
    of strangers—a little dizzy from the fuel fumes
and the stop & go, stop & go, and each time we made

it there early enough so that the beach seemed less crowded,
    smooth white sand already hot underfoot, Santa Maria,
Miramar now called Patricio Lumumbe

after the African martyr. My father taught me to swim
    there; he would hold me flat against the surface
of the water, saying: *"¡Pataléa! Usa los brazos, las manos."*

Use my arms, my hands. Kick. Slowly I got the hang
    of it and I floated, buoyant in the salt and sun,
even though a couple of times I swallowed water

through my nose. Braver, I learned to dunk my head under,
    pinch my nose shut, keep my eyes closed.
To this day, I still do that. My father taught me how

to dive off the crab-infested rock jetties. Then one day
    another kid loaned me a scuba mask and I looked
under the water for the first time, and I saw them, urchins,

scattered on the bottom, like some lost treasure spilled
    from a chest, moving only with the tug
and ebb of the tides, prickly in their armor. Some red,

others black, and my father warned me not to step
        on one, that it would hurt like hell to get one of those spikes
in my foot, so I kept my distance. Saw polka-dotted damsel

fish, the red-green parrot wrasse—of course, I didn't know
        the names of any of these creatures back then,
but I loved the way they swam next to me. Once,

a nurse shark swam by, and I reached out to touch
        its skin so rough, gritty like everything else
on that beach. My father would lay on the sand to catch

some sun; I waded in the surf not too far from him,
        the sun warming the skin on my forehead and shoulders.
My mother has pictures of those days, the skinny kid

leaning against his tall father, of that beach, of the shimmering
        surface of the water, and out on the horizon the barges
I learned later were filled with urchins, thousands of them,

dragged out, exposed, dying in the sun, much like what would
        happen to us in our own country, those of us called
gusanos, the dissidents, those who quickly learned to live with less,

in exile, for another forty years. I look at that picture
        of the urchin slaughter and my eyes burn,
burn because I understand what it means to be away

from the waters we call home.

Landscape with Hawks

In the acre yard of our new home, a pair of hawks
have built a nest high in an oak tree. Now the rest

of the wildlife in the surroundings live in constant
fear. They know what the blanketlike shadow means.

The frogs in the pond nestle deep in grass and weeds,
an islet of hope in the middle of our pond. The turtles,

snakes, eels, salamanders seek refuge under the hyacinth—
days pass when they can only peek from the water

hyacinth leaves, or at night, but then the owls
are out, too, bats, other nocturnal predators. Safety

is the new word. But the hawks, because they have nested,
laid an egg, incubated it, and now rear an ever-growing

chick, the business of scavenge their only intent.
The squirrels live terrified. They too have learned

to cope, duck under a tree stump for cover, or a fallen
branch, under the canopy of azalea bushes. They

traverse the expanse of the yard as if in slow motion.
They are like children who have learned to look both ways

before they cross the street. Mostly, they question
all shadows, to make sure nothing bad ever happens.

And the hawks, they pluck two or three
squirrels a day. This is their duty. My wife and I

admire their persistence. I argue they have it too easy.
I would like for the squirrels to adapt better, play

a trick or two, maybe mutate into larger rodents,
a little bigger and heavier, maybe grow some camouflage

fur, or become slick so that the hawk's talons slip off.
Yes, a race of marine squirrels which have learned

to swim so they can run into the pond for dear life,
dive in and under, and not lose it as they scatter

around the pond's periphery. I want the squirrels
to win, to put their hands to their cheeks and go

"Nyah-Nyah-Nyah" and stick their tongues out at the hawks.
Mockery is good, I say. I know in nature this is the daily

exchange: in order for one creature to survive, another
has to give up its life. So let the hawk have its way,

the squirrels perish until further notice, for now everything
on our property finds survival in the safety of numbers.

Zapper

To spare our daughter any emotional
damage or hardship, my wife and I
often step out to the screened porch
to argue the "little accumulations,"
the times we have wronged each other,
the predawn chill of fighting, and we sit
on these wrought-iron rockers
my father once bought when he thought
he would make time to enjoy them on his own
porch, and we sit and smoke and converse
in low voices, address our grievances,
the silences punctuated by insects
flying into the bug zapper blue realm
as though hypnotized, a kind of lighthouse
of fake longing, and then ZAP!
They drop like minuscule flecks, feathers.
In this courtyard of dogs, we bury
our meaning like bones, in nether regions,
this sacred ritual of accusations, semantics,
the froth of simmered talk, mouthed words,
barks really, like these wire-meshed chairs,
these glyphs imprinted on our thighs
and forearms, the dialogue of clouds,
bad language, verbal middle fingers.
In the meantime, more bugs get sizzled.
Mosquitoes, gnats, flies, bees, wasps,
and the moths. I care about the moths,
crinoline specters tapping their Morse code
with waxy wings against the mesh
of blue-lit zapper, a distress
call, this flit against the wire,
like our argument then, now, again.
Nothing will be resolved, nothing
accomplished, but in the morning

there will be plenty of evidence,
a mound of insects sacrificed
during the wake of our reunion.

II

Cancionero / Songs

Song to the *Cucuyo*

caught them at sundown in the tall grass
by the plantain plants by the porch

of our house in Havana, put several
in clear marmalade jars, brought them

inside the house, as pets, for the night.
There on the nightstand, in the dark,

they flashed their incendiary illuminations,
flashes of fluorescence, like faint lights

of a distant tarmac to signal the passing
of fears, such fears that keep children

awake for so long: old men in cold rooms
sit in the dark, stained undershirts,

the sound of phlegm, fingers gone yellow
from cigarette smoking. This long, long

road through distant cities, wrapped
in strange light. Everywhere, *cucuyos,*

from Havana to Tallahassee, to light
this child's way home.

Song to the Sugarcane

At Publix today with my daughters
I spotted the green stalks of sugarcane

tucked under the boxed Holland tomatoes,
ninety-eight cents a stalk. I grabbed the three

left and brought them home. My daughters,
born in the United States, unlike me, stand

in the kitchen in awe as I take the serrated
knife and peel away the hard green layer,

exposing the fibrous, white, pure slices.
"Here," I say, "nothing is ever as sweet as this."

We stand in the kitchen and chew slices
of sugarcane as I tell them this was my candy

when I was a kid growing up in Havana,
this was the only constant sweetness

in my childhood. This delicious, sweet stalk.
You chew on a piece to remember how

to love what you can't have all the time.

Song to the Mango

For years while he lived in Los Angeles,
then later in Hialeah, Florida, my father
didn't eat mangoes. He would come home
from the market with my mother,
and he would tell her he had seen them
on the stands, mangoes imported from Mexico,
flown from Hawaii, but he couldn't eat
them, not those mangoes—it pained him,
he said, "*me duele mucho.*" My friend
Wasabi once asked my father why.
"They're just as good and sweet as Cubans."
And my father flew into a rage, called him a punk,
a blasphemer for making such a statement.
No mango could ever be as delicious
as a Cuban mango. We laughed
at my father's stubbornness, his refusal
to eat a fruit which he obviously loved
because my mother claimed my father
dreamt of mangoes, when as a child he devoured
them by the dozen, their juices trickling
down his chin, their sweet tartness polished
on his lips. And when he died of a massive
heart attack at Palm Springs hospital,
that day the mango fruit cocktail soured
in the cafeteria trays nurses and doctors
who tasted it puckered in distaste, that night
I dreamt mangoes fell off trees, plummeted
to the earth like shot ducks, dead hopes,
and I could finally understand my father's
avoidance, how even fruit too spoils
                    in foreign countries.

Song to the Lizard

master of obfuscation,
life lived on the scurry

among stems and leaves,
a poet of mossy places,

the sun beckons you
to bathe, a warmth of doubt

in its stillness, your tail a lathe,
mean is your greenness

your fanned throat red
signals an unspoken language

of love, your tail coils,
hooks to the links of chain,

all the time there, perched
on the fence. A monk,

a wise man bent on the idea
of calm resolution, a lost

moth for a meal, the fire ants
make tasty morsels,

what has gotten you this far?
Persistence or desire.

Dream on, magician, fool,
traveler in this land of lost causes.

Song to the Passion Fruit

Every day at noon, when the noise
of the streets subsides, the lovers

come to this room, somewhere
in Old Havana, in this country

of lost causes, and they lay next
to each other on an *hamaca,*

a hammock he has strung up
by the window, low so that in it

their bodies resemble the shape
of a canoe, and their sunburned arms

as they dangle over the edge, oars.
They lay there and read what the cracks

on the walls say, these love poems
in peeling flecks of paint, truths

in the patches of damp ceiling tiles.
After lovemaking, they dream

their escapes where so much water
fills their being. A fly balances

itself on the lip of the water bowl,
braving slick porcelain smoothness,

the burning candle flickers in a moment
of breeze as it cries on itself, slowly,

slow like the lovers passing through
in this life. They love in this room,

silent, oblivious. All the while sparrows
have perched on the branches of the fruit

tree that grows on the balcony
outside the lovers' window.

A fruit tree, its knobby roots each day
deeper, twisted into the concrete and wire mesh,

grows up here on the third-story balcony,
where sparrows now perch and preen.

Theirs is as much a history of this place,
where the single fruit the tree has given

will suddenly be plucked by his arm
as it reaches out through the window

from the swing of the hammock. "This,"
he says, "is the fruit to quench our thirst,

the fruit to appease this hunger."
He brings this fruit to his lover, puts

it close to her mouth, watches as she takes
the first bite. Sweet is the juice of oblivion.

She now shares it with him—if they have
to pretend in this empty room,

then they will imagine this is part
of some story about to be told,

at the end of the end of the world
when the last two humans embrace,

seek consolation that like them, nature
has given, and given, a mother to all.

When the fruit is gone and the lovers
kiss, the fly plops into the water,

gives up its life for the sake of the magical.

Song to the Banyan

the wind frustrates itself, held
in the thin leaves, sifted

through the tendril, ropelike
roots of the mighty banyan

stumps of elephant feet, tough
gray skin of a tree that doesn't bend

against strong wind or hurricane—
this one survived Andrew

in Coral Gables, where the Cubans
live now. They grow backwards

into the ground and sprout
more roots. How like exile

to leave such marks on those spots,
the places where life continues

for those in refuge. A hand clutches
any dirt it can call its own.

Song to the Skink

for several seasons now since we've owned
the house in Tallahassee, the same pair
of blue-tailed skinks have built a nest

under a cement slab by the porch deck.
Every year, they find each other—
the red-headed male with its thick

tail and the sleek female—among mounds
of pine needles and broken twigs.
How do they do it? Find each other?

After winter slumber, under a rock,
coiled up in a crack. What brings
them, this same couple, together, year

after year? Their offspring hatch in early
spring, a hundred or so, and when I
throw out the trash, I hear them scurry,

a flash of blue tail, zigzagging under
rotting leaves by the bloomed azaleas.
This is the order of nature, to bring

such creatures together. I have set up
a trap to catch the parents, take them
to the new house we've bought

not far from this one up for sale.
They have become the constant good
luck in our lives. The children like

them, have learned to come out into
the world and depend on sighting
one or two of the babies, maybe even

the parents, sun-bathing by the garden
hose. These are creatures we've learned
to rely on, each spring, when the world

seems intent on giving all of us another chance.

Song to the Old Oak

fire ants build colonies
on the soil around
your trunk where teeth-
like roots show

their nibbling, not the tickle
of feathers but the curse
of termites burrow deeper
each time an inward Braille

on the exposed dried-out
patches of once-young flesh
the woodpecker picks
apart strips of bark

as though they were scabs
or they hollow out nests
this year few leaves
appeared on your branches

what little bloomed
inclement weather took
the squirrel clambered up
and down as though it takes bets

on how much longer
you'll stand or last
two more storms passed
and didn't knock you

down lightning struck
twice neither time did
you in then in the middle
of a clear harvest moon

lit night you fell as though
to heed some calling
the search for final rest
resilience no longer absolute

the slow silent work
of rot finally wore you down
graceful in surrender
complete

Song in Praise of Xanax

What inevitably begins as a tickle on the bottoms
of my feet works its way up my legs as a tingle,

a current so unmistakable. Then, sweat coats
the palms of my hands, forehead and nape

of neck, and I know the panic of such moments
springs from incertitude, that void of not

knowing. Usually these moments plague
the mind at night, when the body most

surrenders to an active mind, asking what now?
What next? The darkness serves up its silence.

Visions emerge from the ceiling: a house on fire,
a man desperate to leave his country, my father,

a cigarette bent in his mouth, a pit dug at the corner
of the street, and live animals herded and thrown

into the fire, the smell of charred flesh, the blinding
billow of smoke. This is the same smoke that clouds

mind and heart, long enough to feel as if the world
is at its end, but during these moments, what saves us

is a little pink pill, trapezoid in shape, as it dissolves
bitter and sharp in the mouth, as it works its magic

tranquility on the brain, quieting everything.
It is after taking one of these little pills that the heart

reverts to a gallop, a type of *paso fino,* after much rumble,
and I think of my mother, a widow now, alone in her

house, and her singing to herself, to me, what she sang
when I hurt myself, bruised a knee or cut a finger:

*Sana, sana, culito de rana; si no sanas hoy, sanarás
mañana.* Xanax gets us through the night. Blessed

cocktail of chemicals, signals like buoys lighting
this perilous journey home through darkness, storm, fire.

Song to Oxtail Stew

My mother's mother, Donatila,
threw tail chunks into the pot
along with ham hocks, sausage,

sofrito made with peppers, garlic,
onion and chicken broth and simmered
the concoction for hours. Vapors

rose to the ceiling rafters, swirling,
and my grandmother sat me
on her lap and read the smoke.

When it said *hambre,* she closed
her eyes, when it said *sequía,*
she held her breath, when it said

tristeza, she clutched her heart.
She knew her stew was ready
when everyone hungry waltzed

into her kitchen, lured by scent
and all the singing of oxtail bones
clanking against the sides of the black pot.

Song to My Daughters

Alex says she wants to go to San Francisco:
        "Hey, hello, world!" shouts Gabi, who is four.
She will go to Miami to visit her grandmothers,

the sky and sun above them an embrace
        as they pretend travel, their tree swing
the aircraft that takes them where they please,

exotic places, enchanted, vine-stitched jungles,
        and as they float above the earth suspended
by disbelief—wild geese honk across the sky—

Gabi waves; Alex shows them a thumbs-up.
        The girls' sing-song voices shimmer
with make-believe, this gravitational pull between

childhood and adulthood, amazed how distance
        in the afternoon is achieved by pretense,
here now, there then: North Pole, Guatemala,

Mexico, India—thirsty, they rush inside the house,
        their cheeks blushed, sweat glossy
on their foreheads. "It's been a good day,"

they chant in unison, a prayer for this moment
        which has made them both road-weary
and tired. They go upstairs, climb in bed,

swallow the night with a yawn of silence.

Song to the Broken-Down Tractor

For years it sat up on cinder blocks in the shade
of a corrugated tin-roofed shed, where sparrows

built shaggy nests, crows and pigeons perched
away from the afternoon heat, next to the well

I was forbidden to go near because I could fall
in, be swallowed by the bottomless darkness

and never be heard from again, but whenever I
visited my maternal grandparents' farm in San Pablo,

Cuba, the place of the red, broken-down tractor
lured me to its rust, its musk of flat tires, these giants

over me with their treads. I ran my hand over them
and felt their secret of grooves, dirt wedged like words

between them; I climbed onto its wide, black seat,
sat behind the wheel and pretended I was plowing

the earth, tilling it, leaving behind music sheet
bars with swollen notes, a song of my childhood

gone unheard by the adults, my own cousins, how,
if I closed my eyes, the tractor pulled me forward.

I drove it right over the well, over rocks, trees—
nothing could have stopped me.

Song to the *Caracoles*

In the mornings of my Cuban childhood,
I found the empty shells of snails in the garden

where my father planted corn, tomatoes, beans
in the shade of the plantain trees, half-buried

as if to keep their ear to the ground for a secret
or two, and I collected them, kept them in my room

on the windowsill, these creamy shells of hiding.
My grandmother said if I put my ear to them

I could hear the waves, but she meant conch
shells, not these I held in my hands like prayer.

With my next-door neighbor Ricardito, I played
caracoles, a game he invented and taught me

by which we took our shells, turned them upside
down and knocked one shell against the other

and whoever's shell tip broke first, lost.
How many afternoons went into the game,

I'll never know, but I never played with my best
ones, the ones with the swirl of white-cinnamon

color, or the big ones, those I held close to my ears
at night when I lay in bed and thought I heard

all the *babosas,* the homeless families of slugs,
parents, children, slithering toward my window,

a multitude in exodus, pleading their return home.

Song to Cryonics

. . . here the fingers, nails soft as moonglow,
grid of pinked lines against the ghostly
vastness of skin, a hair erect, a perseverance
of trees, kudzu malice to cover everything,
there the lips, spoken words mouthed
with great severity, vowed O's, lips muffled,
echoed sounds cupped by the hand, saying:
when I am gone, remember my face, mirrors
of solitude, a walk in a garden where light
floats down, settles on the surface of a pond,
carp ascend from its murky depths to gobble
a ray or two, enough to keep them glowing
through their quiet nights, eyes fluorescent,
beacons to bring the memories of living home.

III

Duende

Study in Shadow

In sepia, the stilted shadow of my father
    (the one taking the photograph?)
in Havana breaks where I stood
    next to the hibiscus, a boy of six,
hair scalloped back into the *Malanguita,*
    a proper boy's style, my mother's
favorite haircut for boys. This is 1968,
    outside the house of light, house
of shade, the world ablaze with protest,
    war, jungle orange poisons.
A smile faked for all time, my father urges
    it onto the lips of this spindly, awk-
ward boy—me—dressed in matched shirt
    and shorts my mother sewed that summer.
Clean, pretty, sadness riddled in my eyes,
    our parrot Chicharo calls out:
"¡Sonrisa!" Smile, my father says behind
    the camera, then the flash of light
which swallows us both—all that remains
    of that boy is the squint of years,
the weight of memories, broken shadows
    of a man, his son, that life in Cuba
bent on the grass, greener with possibility.

Nocturnal

I tapped your window with a key.
Nightly. After work. Sleepless

in Baton Rouge, the restlessness
a snake in my bones. You let me in.

We didn't speak
there in the dark of your efficiency.

You took me by the hand and led
me. Naked, we made love

until the mattress crashed through
the frame and the next-door neighbor

banged for quiet, calling us sinners.
We kept silent and watched

the roaches, black dots that punctuated
our thoughts as they moved up the wall.

Within the hour I was dressed
and out the door, into the sultry

fog of a city, of a place, of this moment
in our lives. We met this way for months,

coiled into these trysts of lust.
Our body heat made condensation

on the windows. You wrote "don't"
with the tip of your finger. I looked

back long enough to see the woman
at the door, herself a creature driven

by the night to those places the heart
drives to ruin, to break hard against

so much longing, so much innocence.

El desespero

my father said he always checked
    his at the door, before entering
the house, his despair, & it was good
    advice he handed down to me,
& he had picked it up from my
    mother's father, my grandfather,
a man who wiped his mud-caked
    boots on the broken blade of machete
he had rigged by the door as a
    scraper, & he hung his hat, gun,
belt behind the kitchen door
    of my grandmother's house before
he entered the rest of the house.
    "Las armas," he'd say, & no man
should ever bring the world
    in which these things were used
into his house. So I find myself
    living in Tallahassee, my own home
& family now & I don't need them,
    my wild, reckless days behind me.
How I punched my way through conflict,
    hurt the people who cared, violence
always at the doorstep of my ways.
    Now I merely enter my house and pay
homage to the cool air conditioning,
    the quiet of the girls' being at school,
the way the dog stays on her mat
    asleep, all good training for when
I'm gone, like my father, from life,
    a life lived so far in constant bowing,
but smiling, *el desespero* checked always,
    like an overcoat, at the door.

Duende

In the torrential downpours, Lorca arrives one night at our house.
A particularly tempestuous night, not only the weather
outside but my father, inside. My father, young then in Havana,

Lorca's age when the great poet was shot, is being driven to drink
and madness by his dissident government views, and Lorca
glides in from the porch shadows, not a drop of rain on him,

not his face, nor his delicate hands. He leaves no mud prints
as he walks into our living room and sits on our worn chintz
sofa. "What news have you of my father?" my father asks the poet.

Lorca looks around, then lights a *cigarillo,* the incandescence of the match's
flame lighting up his eyes. He exhales, then says: "He died thrown
from his horse." True, my father says and runs into another room.

I approach slowly, driven by the smell of brilliantine in the poet's
combed hair. "Tell me about the *duende,* Señor Lorca." He smiles
and aims a puff of smoke at me—it makes my eyes water.

"You think you have it, *Niño*?" he asks. "I don't know," I say. I need
the trembling of this moment, then silence . . . "If you ever leave
this forsaken country," he adds, "you will neither sing nor play music.

"But the duende will haunt you, like this memory of me, sitting here.
Twenty-five years from today, you will live in Tallahassee, Florida,
and it will be raining. I will knock on your door. You will let me in,

"and I will come and sit on your couch. You will ask me what news have I
of your father, and I will say: 'He is where you last left him, on a hospital
bed, dead of a massive coronary.' You will say: 'How useless.' I will say:

"'*Aprende,* the guitars are weeping. Hear them?' We will sit in silence
and listen to the rain pour down on the earth." Poet in crinoline,
you come from remote regions of sorrow and return to the labyrinth:

love, crystal, stone, you vanish down the rivers of the earth to the sea.

In the House of White Light

When my grandmother left the house
   to live with my aunts, my grandfather,

who spent so much time in the sugarcane
   fields, returned daily to the emptiness

of the clapboard house he built
   with his own hands, and he sat in the dark

to eat beans he cooked right in the can.
   There in the half-light he thought of all he had lost,

including family, country, land; sometimes
   he slept upright on that same chair,

only stirred awake by the restlessness
   of his horse. One night during a lightning

storm, my grandfather stripped naked
   and walked out into the fields around

the house saying, *"Que me parta un rayo,"*
   may lightning strike me, and he stood

with his arms out, the hard rain pelting
   his face, and then the bolts fell

about him, and he danced and cradled
   these filaments in his arms, but they

kept falling, these flashes of white light,
   and he ran back inside and brought out

an armful of large mason jars my grandmother
   used for pickling, and he filled them

with fractal light. Like babies, he carried
    the jars inside and set them all about the house,

and the house filled with the immense
    blinding light that swallowed everything,

including the memories of how each nail
    sunk into the wood, the water level rose

in the well, the loss of this country,
    the family who refused to accept him now,

that in this perpetual waking, the world
    belonged to those who believed in the power

of electricity, those moments zapped
    of anguish, isolation, this clean and pure

act of snatching lightning out of heavy air,
    plucking lightning like flowers from a hillside.

Aerial Photography

There, by the silos, see the tractor
on the cinder blocks, the house
of your birth, next to the pigpens
and the barn, the blackbirds
perched on the clothesline,
and the well covered by two-by-fours
& a black tarp, the way they catch
the sun, such iridescence to burn hollows
in the eyes, the Ceiba tree on fire,
the man below it, on the nap,
his leg being devoured by a serpent,
beyond him the fields, the cane swaying
like emerald waves, oxen carts
being loaded, the cutters scattered
in the clearings, beyond them the mill,
the smokestacks with their plumed
calligraphy, and higher now, much
higher, the island becomes a caiman,
higher still: a bone, a key, a fish,
and above in the stratosphere,
an orbit aswirl much like fireflies
illuminating the path of where
they've been, where they are headed,
a fragmented land, a map of the lost,
a myth in the watery eyes of memory.

Langston Hughes in Havana

For Yusef Komunyakaa

Past the *malecón* where the waves
clash & sing against rocks:

a susurrus *danzón;* past the *cafetales,*
the cane fields, the tobacco-laden

bohíos where a man begins with nothing,
where a man begins with his hands.

I, too, am Cuban. *Cubichón jubiláo.*
And the meeting with Nicolas Guillén

in Batabano-Songoro Cosongo, *replican*
los dioses congoses. Jíbaro coloráo,

cimarrón enbembáo. You know
back in Harlem, the American Dream

drags itself through the streets
like some mangled animal frothing

at the mouth, *Mulato espaviláo.*
In Havana, "Heaven is the place

where happiness is." We can all die
here on this island—the *cocodrilo,*

encantáo, charmed by the sweet
song from your lips. The song says

under the weight of so much toil,
"Wave of sorrow, do not drown me now."

The island, Langston, is still ahead,
and somehow we see its glimmering

sands, its never-ending shores, now
trampled by European tourist trash,

Barbarians on the prowl for well-oiled skin
of the *jineteras: blancas, negras, mulatas*—

it doesn't matter, conquest is color-blind.
Here is the *son,* the cha-cha-cha,

the spilt milk of the coconut.
Listen to the *güajiro's décima,*

sing, singing, you come & go, say:
wave of sorrow, take us there.

Wave of sorrow, don't drown us now.

The Great Chinese Poets Visit Havana

Imagine Tu Fu and Li Po, for they have come
    to the island to lecture on the beauty of rice,

the calligraphy of desire, the way a bamboo
    quill shivers in their hands as ink saturates

their longing. They have come to speak
    about the Art of Repetition to other Chinese

who escaped communism in China only
    to relive it here in Cuba. The poets look out

at the waves beyond *El malecón,* the seawall
    against which the waves spill their secrets.

They witness the *balseros,* so many Cuban rafters
    waving good-bye, *adiós,* as they become mere dots

on the horizon, like characters on the paper.
    Here the egret flaps its wing at the caiman,

at the submerged manatee. The river flows
    beyond the dilapidated buildings, a poetry

of crumbling stone; a mango tree grows
    on a third story balcony where birds

perch against this air of parting. They come
    to read the letters being sent from home, read

them and weep, a fluttering of words against
    the faintest of breezes, like the thinnest of papers.

Listen. They travel the island, they witness the resilience,
    they call out for inner strength in the face of scarcity.

Their sweet voices rise and echo over Sierra Maestra;
    the sullen, distraught faces of so many birds do not

honor them, these great men who merely come
    to speak this cryptic language of absence and longing.

The Great Chinese Poets Exchange Two Words

I. *Aquí:* Spanish for "here," the here and now.

If Tu Fu were Cuban, lived as a refugee in Miami,

he would write home to Cuba to his friend Li Po

that the Cubans in Florida have become strange

birds as they drink from a bitter cup, still drunk

on freedom, uneasy about the persistence of exile,

here where nothing seems as it should be. Even water

hides the green of greed. They have become

transfixed to the idea of a return, though there is

no returning. The sudden downpour makes

the kudzu grow and coil around the bitter heart.

"Tomorrow, the high mountains rise between us.

Our course, vague and uncertain." Your friend or foe.

II. *Allá:* Spanish for "over there," in the unattainable distance.

Li Po quotes from Cuba's martyr José Martí,

who called Cuba and Puerto Rico two wings

of the same bird. Cubans outside the island,

leaving all the time, the place has become

a tomb of forgetting. We are all drunk here,

he writes. Send us money, send us medicine,

tell people over there Ted Turner & his CNN,

their bag of lies are wild boars on the stampede

down a hillside—no thatched-roof hut

can withstand such fury. I would make a bramble

gate for you, your return, but only a simple one,

and a simple supper—the market is so far,

and there's nothing to cook with, in, even the wine

is bitter. But in your return there will be jubilation,

we will drink a cup together, you over there, me

here. *Aquí. Allá.* Two words to bridge the gap.

El exilio

White birds over the gray river.
Scarlet flowers on the green hills.
I watch the Spring go by and wonder
if I shall ever return home.
—Tu Fu

After his accident in Hialeah where he worked
        as a coffee packer, my father returned home
from the hospital and sat by the window
        of the room where my mother sewed,
and he watched the world through the two-inch
        window bars, *su prisión,* he called it,
this catatonia of spirit, he sighed,
        breathing with difficulty in the air-
conditioned apartment he shared with my mother,
        and we would talk on the phone once during
the week, and then on Sundays, he spoke little
        of how he felt, often repeating yesterday's
news or how gray the weather hovered in Miami,
        these cumulus clouds of surrender, a bad
omen for those crossing the Florida Straits on makeshift
        rafts, all trying to get to freedom,
and my father would chuckle his ironic laugh over
        the telephone line as if to say few made it,
and indeed when they made it, *pa' que,* he'd say,
        to lose life in the United States, too much
work, not enough money, too little to show for it,
        but he believed in freedom, in how he came
and went out of his house and had no soul
        ask him for papers or where he was going,
like his old life in Cuba, and the language,
        El Inglés, he never learned, only chewing
on a few necessary words like "mortgage,"
        "paycheck," "punch clock," "bills," . . .

the rest all sounding like the barks of mad
    dogs in an alleyway, the rest
like the poetry he lacked in spirit. *El exilio*
    he sighed, did this to him, his life,
and my mother would sew a dress's hem
    and she would stop long enough to tell him
he was wrong, their (our?) lives here
    had been a blessing, even if hard,
even if they were now alone in this apartment
    in Hialeah where my father watched
the children arrive in the yellow buses
    at the school across the street.
He was there when they came, and there when
    they left, his visions of a daily routine,
like clockwork, beyond the barred window,
    his sedentary life without the use
of his hands, and often, he looked at his thin
    fingers, he thought of the crows he ran
over by the roadside in Cuba, when younger,
    where he knew bad luck when he saw it,
the way these scavengers of the earth
    flocked over a rotting carcass of a killed
animal, the way he wanted to scream out
    his bad luck in English now, say "Fuck You!"
to his life, to this life of sitting and waiting.

The Stayer

Simply, my uncle Chicho stayed
    back in Cuba, against the family's
advice, because everyone left

    and he chose to stay, and this act
of staying marked him as "crazy"
    with most of the men, and he stayed

there in a shack behind my aunt's
    clapboard house, sat in the dark
of most days in the middle

    of the packed-dirt floor and nodded
at the insistence of light, the way
    it darted through holes in the tin

roof where the rain drummed
    like the gallop of spooked horses.
This is where he was born, he chanted

    under his breath to no one, why should
he leave, live in perpetual longing
    within exile? He learned long ago

to count the passing of time
    in how motes danced in the shaft
of white light, the *chicharras* echoed

    their trill against the emptiness
of life, against the wake of resistance
    in this place he knew as a child,

as a man, *un hombre,* bent against this idea
     of leaving his country, call him *loco.*
What nobody counted on was that answers

     come only to those who sit in the quiet
of their own countries, tranquil
     in the penumbra, intent on hearing the song

of a *tomegüín* as it calls for a mate
     to come nest in the shrubs out there,
while in here, he witnesses how light

fills the emptiness with the meaning of stay.

Carbon Monoxide Meditations

In memory of Larry Levis

in line at the emissions control center on Miami's Bird Road & 40th,
"Blue Moon" on the radio, your last book *Elegy* on my lap, reading from "In 1967"

and feeling like this day, clear and windy, is a day that cannot be lived otherwise.
I am a runner of existential errands. My father more than a month in the ground,

you also gone from us, this world of rusted chrome, mufflers, and fumes.
Our last time together, I saw you read a poem from this same book,

and I laughed because you opened the reading by dedicating the opening poem
to all the health-food, exercise fanatics "who will die just like the rest of us."

This memory saves me for now, stuck here in this line, fools too used to the art
of hoop-jumping. My father loved these moments, lived for them, but there

was no poetry in his mind or heart. A practical man, he only used language
as the tool by which he lived, asked for things, traded for and lost,

and I read about you, the spraying of fields to kill the waxwing, but we are far
from any fruitful earth here—the earth we all knew, you, him, me. Red dirt,

the kind that clumps to one's boots. We are here, Larry, Father, performing
this yearly task of passing emissions control so we don't pollute

the already-polluted air. I think of California, your home, and you so far from it
in Richmond, Virginia, not necessarily alone, oblivious to the possibility

of no return, like a bird shut out of its nest. Is this all that is left to us? These
existential tasks, the wearing down of the spirit not to a shiny smooth surface

but something dull and coarse like sandpaper, like the prickles on leaves of grass.
We want to rise above all this, this moment of noise, horns, engines on the rev,

lives like mine going up in smoke to kill the ozone. Is this what will happen
if there's a heaven, a long line of souls checking in? Waiting inspection?

"This I know. One day," my father said, "your well will run dry—what
you call remembrance will cease to give up material, and you will have to live

for that which nourishes instantly." Look in the mirror, see the veins in your eyes,
blood vessels, see a pencil-thin scar over an eyebrow—how did it happen?

This blemish upon your beautiful face? A rock, a knife cut, a barroom brawl?
You can turn down your shadow. You can look over your shoulder at fields

spotted with mounds of dead birds. Not an empty field. Not barren either.
Upon closer look, beyond the tilled earth, the rocks. See them, see the big one

with the sparrow perched on its one good foot, the other a bloody stump—
a leg lost to a snake? This is the way so many of us have learned to live in exile,

some part of ourselves lost forever, in this instant. I see you, Larry, on a tractor,
in a field so big and wide, riding this tractor, you are tilling

and furrowing the earth, and from a bird's view, a poetry appears for angels
and mere mortals. It is a long time yet before my father's car passes the test,

and the carbon monoxide has made drunks of us all. The horns begin to sound
their discontent, but for this instant we wait, look up, smile at all the exhaust

induced thoughts going up into the thin air of memory, stuck, saying
this is the last time.

Recitative after Rembrandt's "The Anatomy Lesson of Dr. Tulp"

how the whiteness of flesh beckons the doctor's eyes averted
from the flash of muscle, tendonlike pulleys, rubber
bands useless now in death, and in the brightest light,

the good doctor's hands shine, one holding a pair of tweezers,
the other in explanatory gesture as if to say look how the red
of exposed arteries, darkened in crimson light, contrasts

against corpse-pale, moments when corporeal secrets
still held the curiosity of those gathered to study how the body
works, functions, even in this futility of the laid-out, another

corpse donated by the city morgue, a drunkard, a wayward soul,
and I think of my own father, a hard-working man, dead
of complications in surgery, or rather, how a blood clot choked

his heart into submission, and his eyes closing to the world,
a fluorescence of white doves aflutter on the roof of a train
station, my father a young man of fifteen on the way to Havana

to seek his fortune, and fifty years later, in another country,
in the bark of a foreign tongue, in the whirlwind of exile,
his ears surrender to the sound of a muted cry, his own,

and the hospital's ICU doctors and nurses flock to him, his heart
will not start up again, and they paddle it with electricity, paddle
again, but his heart knows its calling, a Royal Palm tree calls it

home, where the rivers teem with the silver of fish, fiery beings
under the water's mirror, and he wants to go home, he yearns
for this place of his youth, the doctors and nurses stand dumbfounded

because Dr. Tulp, despite a lifetime of practice and a steady
hand, is too late; science has failed him, my father, as science fails us all.

Atmospheric

Every night I go to bed here in Austin
so far from family and when I remove

my glasses, the ceiling turns into constellations,
mercurial lights. Tonight is the night, I say

to myself, everything ends: the irregular beat
of my heart, its murmur audible on the pillow.

This whir and the skips of arrhythmia, clap
of some distant drum, out there beyond

my heart, beyond this body, falling apart.
In another galaxy, surely somebody lies

on his back, gives up the ghost of this haunting—
out there: a wife, a couple of lovely

daughters living on, away from the longing
of my hands, hands that clutch a heart

too weak to survive the furies of the distances
between the living and the dead, a wakefulness

from which exists no escape, no surrender.
Awake in Austin, night, a heart sings its rapture.

Middle Ground, or *El camino del medio*

my father always spoke of what he had forgotten
about Cuba, his homeland, how the specifics
blurred, and he blamed this condition
on the in-betweenness of spirit that occurs
in immigrants, those who live in exile
in the United States, and then he uttered
some words of English, "Mortgage," "Time
Clock," "Payday," these words he had learned
out of necessity, and he couldn't remember
all the jobs he held in Cuba before he arrived
in the United States. He sat in his reclinable
cushioned chair (doctor-recommended)
because after his accident he felt useless,
his hands he always looked at and called his
pajaritos muertos, his dead birds, a man filled
with burnt-out memories of the neither
here nor there, a mind cluttered with debris
of daily life, bills, errands, responsibilities,
and when he stared out the bedroom
window where he sat all day, he thought
of the rivers, the valleys, cane fields
of his childhood, atop a horse he rode,
straddled tight, over into the horizon,
no longer a man afflicted with the idea
of middle, no in-between, no refuge, absence.

Diaspora

For Nancy Morejón

To tell the truth
I used to think the word
meant some kind of fungus

like the mold that attacks bread,
something that survives a hostile
environment, no matter.

You say that the word
cannot embrace those Cubans
who left the island to seek

refuge elsewhere, many in cold
places, that the word only applies
to the cruel punishment inflicted

on African slaves. Okay. But
I have seen Cubans everywhere,
scattered from Tierra del Fuego

to Iceland. I have seen the ones
perishing in snow, these wounded
fish and when I look into their eyes,

Nancy, like when I look into yours,
I see the possibility of reconciliation,
not the fixed gaze of hatred, but like mold

we have taken root where the wind threw
us, like these persistent and determined
growths, we will prevail. We hang on.

The longing in our faces cannot end
until both shores unite, yours and mine,
the sting of these subtle twists of definitions.

My Paternal Grandmother's Instructions Before We Left Cuba

If we flew, not to look at the clouds too long, they spoke too much anger.

If we sailed, seawater could never show us the way, stars would.

When upon free soil, bow to the four directions to pay the wind homage.

When asked for papers, show the fire in our hands, how charmed the flames play.

In traffic, take off our red shirts or skirts and scream *"¡Ah-Ha! ¡Toro! ¡Olé!"*

Beware of used furniture: a worn sofa swallows not only money, but luck.

In times of plenty, serve an extra plate, always with rice.

In times of scarcity, think of the old country, do not mistake "want" for "lack."

Never look into a mirror that reflects another mirror or get lost in infinity.

Leave the front door always open, a horseshoe nailed to the inside archway.

Speak of how much water the sky gave the earth.

How seeds seek light after a dark spell.

In springtime, open the windows of our new house, invite the birds to feed.

In the fall, always leave a glass of water under the bed.

Watch for how dust gathers in corners.

At night when we close our eyes to sleep, think of her as a gardenia flower.

Think of her as an open hand waving good-bye atop her grave.

Adiós, Adiós, Adiós

you can hear it, the clock,
its intricate whir of parts,
it knows what time it is,
but refuses to chime.

The century, its caravan
of years, winds down,
Conestoga wagons
on the trail, canvas tops

aflame, dust from its
hold kicks up ghosts,
a century of illusions,
hocus-pocus medicine

and magic. Only crows
know the real meaning
of the universe, how it begins
with iridescence

like their plumage, slick
rainbow of possibility.
It flies into a tunnel,
the flapping of wings

mark the pace, warn
us the ride's coming
to an end. Close your eyes,
feel the wiggle in the belly,

hold onto your hat.
Lots of rough air ahead.

About the Author

Virgil Suárez was born in Havana, Cuba, in 1962. He is the author of four published novels: *Latin Jazz, The Cutter, Havana Thursdays,* and *Going Under,* and of a collection of short stories entitled *Welcome to the Oasis.* With his wife, Delia Poey, he has co-edited two best-selling anthologies: *Iguana Dreams: New Latino Fiction* and *Little Havana Blues: A Contemporary Cuban-American Literature Anthology.* Most recently he has published an anthology of Latino poetry titled *Paper Dance,* co-edited with Victor Hernández Cruz and Leroy V. Quintana, and his own collection of poetry and memoir titled *Spared Angola: Memories From a Cuban-American Childhood.* He is the author of three previous collections of poems: *You Come Singing, Garabato Poems,* and *In the Republic of Longing.* His poetry, stories, and essays continue to appear in national reviews and journals such as *The Kenyon Review, Ploughshares, The New England Review, The Massachusetts Review, The Mississippi Review,* and *Quarterly West.* He is also the translator of Colombian poet Juan Carlos Galeano's book of poetry entitled *Amazonia.* A frequent book reviewer, his reviews appear in *The Los Angeles Times, The Miami Herald,* and *The Philadelphia Inquirer.* Recently he has served as panelist/adviser to the National Endowment for the Arts, The Oscar B. Cintas Foundation, and The Lila Wallace Reader's Digest Award. He divides his time between Miami and Tallahassee, where he lives with his family.

Source Acknowledgments

Grateful acknowledgment is made to the editors and publishers of the following reviews and journals where some of these poems first appeared, sometimes in a slightly different form: *Albatross, Apalachee Quarterly, Cedar Hill Review, Concho River Review, Controlled Burn, Crab Creek Review, Crazyhorse, Grain* (Canada), *Habersham Review, Leapings Literary Review, Membrane, Mockingbird, New Delta Review, New Orleans Review, Other Poetry* (England), *Oxford Magazine, Oregon East, Paris / Atlantic* (France), *Peer Poetry Review* (England), *Pembroke Magazine, Piedmont Literary Review, Pleiades, Ploughshares, International Poetry Review, Poet Lore, Potomac Review, Prairie Schooner, Quarterly West, Queen's Quarterly* (Canada), *Red Rock Review, River Styx, Sow's Ear Poetry Review, Tampa Review, Tameme, Tempus, The American Voice, The Caribbean Writer, The Metropolitan Review, The Marlboro Review, The Raven's Chronicle, The New England Review, The Comstock Review, Washington Square, Westview, Willow Review,* and *Windsor Review* (Canada).

Works by Virgil Suárez

Fiction

The Cutter
Latin Jazz
Havana Thursdays
Going Under
Welcome to the Oasis (a novella & stories)

Poetry

Spared Angola: Memories From a Cuban-American Childhood
You Come Singing
Garabato Poems
In the Republic of Longing
Café Nostalgia: Writings from the Hyphen
Gusano
Amazonia (translation)

Anthologies

Iguana Dreams: New Latino Fiction
Paper Dance: 55 Latino Poets
Little Havana Blues: A Contemporary
Cuban-American Literature Anthology
Is There a Boom in Latino Literature?
American Diaspora: Poetry of Displacement
Like Thunder: Poets Respond to Violence in America
Clockpunchers: Poetry of the American Work Place